SNIPPETS

Memories to Enhance Healing, Health, and Wellness

JOSEPH N. DELUCA, MD, PH.D.

BALBOA.
PRESS

A DIVISION OF HAY HOUSE

Balboa Press books may be ordered through booksellers or by contacting:

Balboa Press
A Division of Hay House
1663 Liberty Drive
Bloomington, IN 47403
www.balboapress.com
1 (877) 407-4847

Because of the dynamic nature of the Internet, any web addresses or links contained in this book may have changed since publication and may no longer be valid. The views expressed in this work are solely those of the author and do not necessarily reflect the views of the publisher, and the publisher hereby disclaims any responsibility for them.

The author of this book does not dispense medical advice or prescribe the use of any technique as a form of treatment for physical, emotional, or medical problems without the advice of a physician, either directly or indirectly. The intent of the author is only to offer information of a general nature to help you in your quest for emotional and spiritual well-being. In the event you use any of the information in this book for yourself, which is your constitutional right, the author and the publisher assume no responsibility for your actions.

Any people depicted in stock imagery provided by Thinkstock are models, and such images are being used for illustrative purposes only.
Certain stock imagery © Thinkstock.

ISBN: 978-1-4525-8731-8 (sc)
ISBN: 978-1-4525-8732-5 (e)

Printed in the United States of America.

Balboa Press rev. date: 11/26/2013

DEDICATION

I dedicate this book to my parents, Joseph and Angela. My dad was my inspiration for hard work and perseverance. As a youngster, when he went to work as an auto mechanic, he would leave the house early in the morning and return late at night. I would ask my mother how was he able to do that, wouldn't he be too tired after working so many hours? She replied that "he just had to do what he had to do". My dad was extremely skillful with his hands and when we moved from New York City to the suburbs, when I was in the 8th grade, he single handily built in our house, two bedrooms and a bathroom upstairs, and a year later added a family room downstairs, and several years later added an upper deck to the second floor. Although he was kind of a "tough guy", he was extremely affectionate, loving, caring, and gentle to my mother, brother, sister, and myself.

He was 5' 9" and weighted 210 lbs., of sold muscle. He would mention how he and a friend of his could lift 100 lbs., with one hand, over their heads several times. I thought, wow, I never wanted to be hit by him. He admired strength and speed. During High School football practice, I apparently was winning all of the wind sprints, so the track coach asked me to try out for track. When he timed me he said I had sprinter speed, I could not wait to get home and tell my father, I was a "sprinter". He didn't say a word; he smiled and nodded, and came to several of my track meets that year. Years later when he passed away I put several of the track metals that he saw me win in his pocket. I thanked him for being a great Dad and for passing on the genes permitting me to run really fast. I also discovered, later in life, that I also had inherited his genes for physical strength.

My mother was the essence of a right brain person in that she had a great flare for design, color, fashion and the ability to perseive spactial relationships very well. She digested a book every two weeks from The Book of the Month Club, and was always reading magazines on design and fashion. The caption under my mother's picture in her highschool Yearbook read "A summarized version of charm, personality, and wit." Now that's a tough act to follow. Despite growing up during the Depression both of my parents finished two years of college even though they each worked three part-time jobs while attending college, my father as an Engineering major and my mother as an English/History major. Years later, after my father passed away, she worked as an interior decorator. My mother was a very soft, gentle, loving person. She was proud to admit, however, that in college she once got a "B" in calculus, so the left side of her brain was no slouch either. When she and my father would come to some of my football games whenever she thought I was going to be hit while running with the ball she would close her eyes. On those occasions when she did not have time to close her eyes she would ask my father, "is it necessary that they have to hit him so hard"? Yes, she was a smidgen overprotective, but it was ladled with tons of unconditional love.

So, thank you God for giving me two wonderful, loving, bright parents.

SNIPPETS
MEMORIES TO ENHANCE HEALING, HEALTH & WELLNESS

A snippet, as defined here, consists of a few words, which when a person looks at them, usually brings forth a flood of memories, images, or fantasies. The idea is for a person to sit or lie down, and look at a "snippet" and relive or replay the moments that the snippet stimulates. The ideal way to do this is to write down what the fantasy or memory was that the particular snippet stimulated, so that in time you will accumulate a vast array of past experiences that correlate with a given snippet.

It is true that a given snippet can elicit a bittersweet memory, such as the loss of a loved one, but that can help the healing process, especially when one can focus on the precious moments together as well as the heartache of the loss.

Many of the snippets are designed to bring forth memories of experiences that require continued healing. By replaying past experiences that were painful the individual continues to reintegrate them in a way that makes them less painful or traumatic. Therefore, snippets that precipitate memories of painful experiences are important for self-healing, as the reintegration process continues.

Ego strength is built, in good part, by experiences of success and satisfaction and by replaying, each day, these kinds of experiences, by way of a snippet, ego strength is enhanced. Just as a person does a physical workout to enhance physical well-being, a snippet is a kind of emotional workout that enhances health and wellness.

It is recommended that a person do three positive "snippets" for every negative "snippet". This is important so that the negative emotion does not dominate over the positive emotions. If you find that a particular negative "snippet" produces a profound emotional distress and pain that qualifies you for having replayed an experience that is a post traumatic stress disorder type, it is crucial that you work with a psychologist or counselor in dealing with that particular memory.

By all means one is encouraged to come up with their own "snippets", those words, which for them, provoke extreme joy and/or memories of past hurts.

THESE ARE THE "SNIPPETS" THAT WILL HELP REPLAY THE POSITIVE EXPERIENCES THAT CONTRIBUTE TO EGO STRENGTH

FAIRYTALES & LULLABY'S

A FIRESIDE

INNER BEAUTY

CHRISTMAS MORNING

FULFILLMENT

I CAN'T STOP THINKING ABOUT YOU

A Time For Us

Holding Hands

An Achievement

APPROVAL

I NEVER GAVE UP

BAREFOOT ON THE BEACH

DANCING

GRADUATION

BEAUTIFUL MORNING

GRANDPA

YOU WERE MY INSPIRATION

BEING SO BLESSED

BELIEVING

FIRST DATE

BLISS

GARDENIAS & MAGNOLIAS

YOU NEVER GAVE UP ON ME

OUR FAMILY

I Can Always Keep On Going

Celebration

It was so Romantic

Joseph N. Deluca, MD, Ph.D.

FROM THE LIGHT

YOU SHOWED ME WHAT UNCONDITIONAL LOVE WAS ALL ABOUT

COOL MIST

COPPERTONE

GRANDMA

DAYDREAMS

DO IT FOR ME

YOU MADE ME FEEL SO LOVED

FIRST DANCE

DRIFTING

GENTLENESS

EROICA – BEETHOVEN

I Will Never Give Up

Euphoria

A Beautiful Face

FEELING GRATEFUL

FEELING SILLY

TOGETHER AGAIN

Joseph N. Deluca, MD, Ph.D.

First Love

Sweet Music

I Couldn't Stop Laughing

FLASHES OF HOPE

NEW YEAR'S EVE

FOREVER

I Was Mesmerized

Sweet Soothing Music

Gentle Breeze

BEAUTIFULLY SIMPLE

GENTLE FALLING SNOW

GOING HOME

GOOD NEWS

DREAMING OF YOU

I REACHED FOR YOU

My Old Flame

My Heaven

First Kiss

Joseph N. Deluca, MD, Ph.D.

ACCEPTANCE

GREGORIAN CHANT

KITTENS

HEALING

IT IS VERY QUIET THERE

MY WILD FLOWER

HOLDING BABIES

ALMOST HEAVEN

HOLDING, HUGGING, & KISSING

I am Grateful for ...

Music From The ...

Being Healed by You

Joseph N. Deluca, MD, Ph.D.

PRETTY GIRL

YOU LIFT ME UP

BEAUTILICIOUS

I Forgive ...

A Quite Place

My Squishalicious

Joseph N. Deluca, MD, Ph.D.

I Searched for ...

My Light

I Was There

KITTENS

TASTES REALLY GOOD

FLOWING WATER

BEST FRIEND

A PRECIOUS MOMENT

MY WISH

Into the Light

It Was Magic

Beautiful Day

JUST PERFECT

FLOATING

KNOWING YOU

FIRST PROM

LEARNING TO LISTEN

PURE INNOCENCE

LETTING IT ALL HANG OUT

FOREVER IN MY HEART

LIGHT

Listening to the Silence

Long Ago

Soft Summer Breeze

LOVING YOU

MEDITATING

PUPPIES

MEMORIES

FIRST PLACE

MOUNTAIN AIR

SUMMER VACATION

SO GRACEFUL

MY BEST FRIEND

MY CUTIE WOOTIE

SOFT GUITAR MUSIC

BURNING LEAVES

My First Medal

Toys, Ice Cream & Cookies

My Gardens

So Full of Joy

My Honey Bun

My Incredible Journey

Joseph N. Deluca, MD, Ph.D.

MY INSPIRATION

SLOWING DOWN TIME

TENDER

YOU WERE SWEET TO ...

TRIUMPHS

GETTING MARRIED

Joseph N. Deluca, MD, Ph.D.

I'M DETERMINED TO ...

MY WILDEST DREAM

THE PROMOTION

ICE CREAM

NEVER, EVER, GIVE UP

NEW DAY

Joseph N. Deluca, MD, Ph.D.

OH MY! OH MY! OH MY!

THAT SPECIAL MOMENT

ONE OF A KIND

THINKING OF YOU

BLUE SKY

OUTRAGEOUSLY SEXY

PASSING MY DRIVING TEST

I'M JUST GETTING STARTED

STARS

PLEASE BE HERE

ANDREA BOCHELLI

MY ANGEL

I Really Earned it

Promises

The Team

MY OWN BED

INTENSELY CALM

PURE SERENITY

REFLECTIONS

THE FRESH START

RIDING MY BIKE

SLEIGH RIDING

SO CUTE

MY TIME FOR HEALING

So Forgiving

So Tranquil & Peaceful

My Comfort Zone

THANKSGIVING

MY DREAMS

THE LAKE

Soft Rain

Old Friends

Solitude

PREVIOUS LIVES

STARLIGHT

STAYING IN THE MOMENT

TRUE LOVE

STRETCHING

YOU OPENED MY HEART

THE GOOD TEACHER

SUMMERS AT THE BEACH

SUNRISE

Joseph N. Deluca, MD, Ph.D.

WOW, THAT WAS GREAT

SUNSET

SWAYING

PEACEFUL

SWEET SWEET CHILD

TWO HEARTS

Joseph N. Deluca, MD, Ph.D.

TENACITY

PLAYING WITH PETS

THAT ONE SPECIAL MOMENT

THAT REALLY HELPED

THROUGH THE YEARS

THAT WAS SO THOUGHTFUL

Joseph N. Deluca, MD, Ph.D.

Remember When

The Announcement

I Believe That ...

THE AROMA OF ....

THE AROMA OF INNOCENCE

THE AROMA OF WELLNESS

THE CHALLENGE

WHO INSPIRED ME

THE GOOD CIGAR

THE INSIGHT

BEAUTY

THE JOURNEY

YOUR HEALING TOUCH

THE MESSAGE

THE MILKY WAY

THE MOMENT

THE PARK

THE PATH TO ...

SOFT MUSIC

THE SOUND OF WATER

SUMMER AT THE SHORE

THE THRILL OF ...

RESTING

THE WONDERFUL OPPORTUNITY

Too Cute

Total Relaxation

True Friend

WAS IT OK?

THE LOOK OF LOVE

WINNING

A MOUNTAIN TOP

YOU ARE SO COMFORTING

SPIRITUAL

THESE ARE THE "SNIPPETS" THAT WILL HELP WITH EXPERIENCES THAT REQUIRE HEALING

I Wish I Hadn't

Savage and Brutal

Beaten

Joseph N. Deluca, MD, Ph.D.

THE MISSED OPPORTUNITY

I WAS SO HUMILIATED

DAMN DAMN

76

BEING RIDICULED

FEELING LOST

GETTING BULLIED

BETRAYED

THE LIE(S)

HOMELESS

BAD NEWS

HOW COULD YOU ...

THE LONELINESS OF ...

GOING TO JAIL/PRISON

I CRIED WHEN ...

THE LONG GOOD-BYE

FAREWELL

WOUNDED

I FELT DESTROYED

THE DREADED ENCOUNTER

I FELT SO ASHAMED

9-11

THAT WAS SO CRUEL

TOTALLY LOST

I STILL CAN'T GET OVER ...

I Was so Ashamed

I Was so Bitter

Getting Divorced

Worried Sick

I Will Never Let it Go

Misunderstood

Joseph N. Deluca, MD, Ph.D.

IF ONLY I HAD ...

THE PAIN OF ...

IT WAS REPULSIVE

THE UNBEARABLE LOSS

MY BIGGEST MISTAKE

I DID NOT ...

Joseph N. Deluca, MD, Ph.D.

UNFAITHFUL

I AM SORRY FOR ...

MY HEART ACHES

My Secret(s)

Wounded

Picked Last

Joseph N. Deluca, MD, Ph.D.

I Just do not Understand ...

So Far Away

You Have Cancer

STARVING CHILDREN

THAT REALLY HURT

I FELT SO LONELY WHEN ...

THE HUMILIATION

I FELT LOST

THERE WAS NO JUSTICE

I so Wanted Revenge

I Didn't Deserve That

So Impatient

ACKNOWLEDGEMENTS

I would like to acknowledge the help of my wife, Dr. Penny DeLuca for her advice regarding editing, formatting, front cover design and overall enthusiastic support. In addition, I would like to acknowledge Nucci Cento for her continued support in my endeavor to write a workbook that would be helpful to people to enhance their mental health and wellbeing. I would also like to thank Karen Boble for her continued efforts in retyping the manuscript until I got it correct.